Just Think!

Good Apple

Senior Editor:
Donna Borst

Cover Design:
Signature Design Group, Inc.

GOOD APPLE
A Division of Frank Schaffer Publications, Inc.
23740 Hawthorne Blvd.
Torrance, CA 90505

GA1653 ISBN 1-56417-984-2

3 4 5 6 7 8 9

Table of Contents

To the Teacher

Just Think! is a compilation of past issues of *Challenge* magazine, which has been in gifted classrooms all over the world for over 16 years. After all of this time, we looked back at the wonderful material sitting on our shelves and decided it was time to share the wealth of ideas that have accumulated over the years. *Challenge* has long been known for its innovative, creative ideas, and we felt those ideas were just too good to waste. After sifting through 75 issues, we have come up with the best of the best creative thinking ideas and have compiled them into one terrific resource for the gifted classroom.

One great thing about *Challenge* is that every idea, activity, and unit has been written by teachers or parents just like you. These are people who know what works in a classroom and what doesn't. They know about the uniqueness of gifted children and how to motivate and stimulate them.

If you have ideas that you would like to share with other teachers or parents through *Challenge* magazine, we would love to hear from you. You may submit your ideas to *Challenge*, 3427 Pheasant Run Drive, Wever, IA 52658. If you would like to subscribe to *Challenge*, please call 1-800-264-9873.

Other books compiled from *Challenge* magazine:
GA1652 *Adventures in the Gifted Classroom*

The Case of the Disappearing Car

Witnesses can play a big role in solving a crime, so detectives are always eager to question people who might have seen something important. Sometimes a situation may be so baffling, however, that the evidence from witnesses seems impossible. Creative people have to work out ways to show how the facts realistically fit together. Consider the following scenario.

The police know that two robbers have escaped in a small white car. Two witnesses report that they saw it turn onto their street, Long Lane, at 3:00. Since the witnesses remained seated in their yard watching the street for several hours, they are certain that the small white car never turned around and came back out. They testified that two or three other cars went down the street and also never returned, but they could not recall the colors.

Long Lane winds around a small lake. The lake is on one side, and open spaces, a wooded area, and a few houses are on the other side. There are no side roads leading off Long Lane.

At the other end of this street two more witnesses have been busy outside because they have been packing and moving their belongings. One or the other of these two witnesses has been working in the street from 3:00 to 5:00 because they have had to guide traffic around the large moving truck they are using. They report that only three cars have passed—a black car, a red one, and a blue one. There has been no white car.

The police have found that the white car is no longer on Long Lane. How could it have disappeared? Where could it have gone—and how? In a science-fiction story, it might have been beamed up into a space ship. In a ghost story, the car might have been a phantom, but this story is based on everyday life. A good imagination is required in order to find realistic solutions to seemingly impossible situations. How many ways can you explain the disappearance of a car?

After you've thought of several possibilities, check your solutions against those of other young mystery lovers. Remember that in a real mystery story, every character is under suspicion until the answers are found, so give the characters different roles. Each idea you have could be the basis for a full story, and each one would be entirely different because of the actions and motives of the various people involved.

Possible Solutions to the Disappearing Car

1. Some of the witnesses did not report the true facts.
   a. Maybe the two people at the beginning or the two people at the end of Long Lane lied in order to mislead the police.

   b. Maybe the witnesses at the beginning of Long Lane were mistaken—no white car ever entered their street.

   c. Maybe one of the witnesses at the end of the street simply missed seeing the car leave Long Lane.

2. The car's appearance has been changed in some way.
   a. Maybe the thieves carried cans of spray paint. They were able to stop along the road and quickly cover the car with red, black, or blue paint.

   b. Maybe the car was really a darker color and it had been whitewashed. The thieves were able to wash away the white paint with the water from the lake and drive a blue car past the other witnesses.

3. The car is still there, but it is carefully hidden.
   a. Maybe the thieves hid the car in the wooded areas along the road.

   b. Maybe the thieves pushed the car into the lake.

   c. Maybe the car is hidden inside the garage of one of the houses.

   d. Maybe the car is inside the moving van. The witnesses at the end of Long Lane may actually be the thieves, and they feel certain the police will not think about looking inside the truck.

Were you able to think of any other possibilities? A "disappearing car" seems unbelievable, but creative people are able to make "impossible" things happen.

Are You a Good Detective?

Locked rooms provide one of the most challenging puzzles for mystery readers and writers. The situation seems impossible: How can a crime be committed in a room that no one can enter or exit?

Creative minds come up with many different answers. Read over the following scenario and see how many possibilities you can imagine. Use only realistic ideas. Fantasy, magic, or gadgets from science fiction are not permitted.

The Disappearing Diamond

Mr. Jones, a very wealthy man, has bought an expensive diamond. He says that he's worried that someone might steal the jewel before he can get it to his bank safety-deposit box in the morning.

"I have this room with no windows in my home," he tells Mr. Smith. "I would like to put my diamond on the middle of a table in the middle of this empty room and then lock the only door. Someone needs to remain outside the locked door all night to make sure no one gets inside. Would you guard the door for me?"

Mr. Smith says he would be glad to act as a guard. "You can depend on me," he tells Mr. Jones. "I'll make sure no one gets in or out of that room."

And so Mr. Jones puts his diamond on the middle of the table. He and Mr. Smith leave the windowless room. They lock the only door behind them. "Here's the key," Mr. Jones says.

Mr. Smith puts the key in his pocket. He sits down on a chair by the locked door. "No one will get past me," he promises.

The next morning Mr. Jones comes back. Mr. Smith is still sitting where he left him. "No one went in or out," he says. "I sat here all night drinking coffee, so you can be sure no one stole your jewel."

"Good!" Mr. Jones takes the key from him and unlocks the door. He hurries over to the table, then turns around and shouts, "But the diamond is gone! Someone did steal it!"

- Who might have stolen the diamond?
- How was it done?
- Think of as many possibilities as you can, and then compare your ideas with those other writers have had.

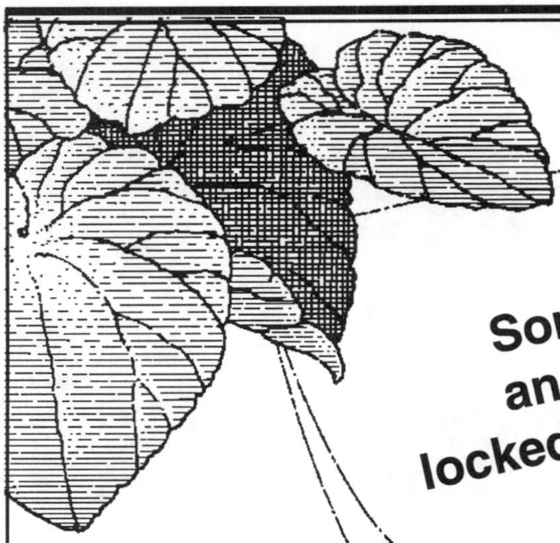

Some possible answers to the locked room robbery...

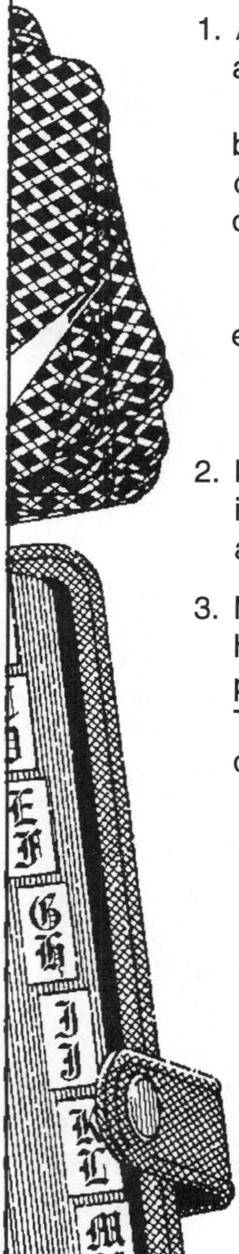

1. An outsider may have stolen the diamond.
   a. Maybe the thief came in through an underground tunnel and entered through a trapdoor in the floor.
   b. Maybe the thief came down through a skylight in the roof.
   c. Maybe the thief entered the room through an air vent.
   d. Maybe there is a secret panel in the room. The thief was hiding behind the panel when the men left the diamond, and he is still hiding there now. He'll leave when the men hurry to call the police.
   e. Maybe the thief drugged the guard's coffee, took the key, and went through the door while Mr. Smith slept. Mr. Smith was either not aware that he had slept, or he was too embarrassed to admit it.

2. Mr. Smith, the guard, stole the diamond. This answer is possible, but it seems unlikely since he was still waiting there when Mr. Jones arrived.

3. Mr. Jones stole his own diamond. This answer is possible because he may have run to the table and grabbed up his own jewel and pocketed it before Mr. Smith was able to see what he was doing. Then Mr. Jones would be able to collect the insurance for his "stolen" diamond even though he would still have the jewel.

Were you able to think of any other possibilities? The best thing about writing mysteries is that there is no ONE way to solve them. As long as the answer is feasible, every writer can come up with his or her own solutions to baffling puzzles. This is the way plots are created.

Can you think of any other mysterious things that could happen in an empty, windowless, locked room?

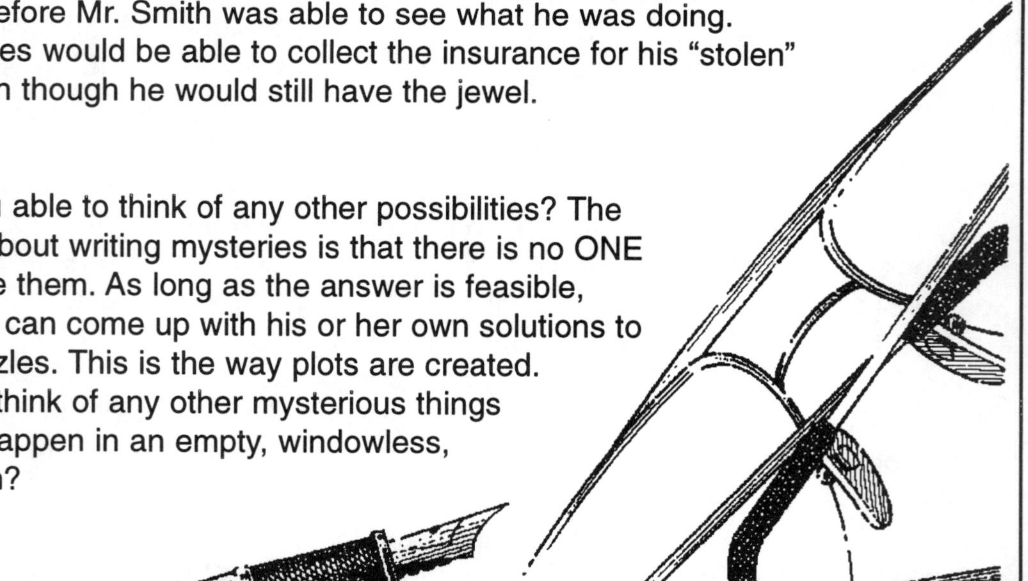

Youth Sleuths on the Loose!

Mystery writers often use kids as detectives because child characters can ferret out clues that adults occasionally overlook. By being quietly observant, children can discover answers to baffling puzzles. Test your own ability to solve a mystery with the following plot idea.

Imagine that you're a young detective who has learned that a prisoner has escaped from the local jail in a small Michigan town. You're about to take a car ferry across Lake Michigan to Wisconsin, and you suspect this man might try to get on board. You know the man is short and thin, so you stand on the dock and watch very carefully as the boarding process begins. Everyone else is too busy to notice anything other than their own activities.

First, the crew members, dressed in gray uniforms, drive the passenger cars into the ship's hold. Next, they carry in various barrels, boxes, and cartons. After the cargo is loaded, the captain and three officers come on board. They are followed by these passengers:

- A short, plump man in sunglasses and a jogging suit.

- A tall thin man who has two crew members helping him. They are carrying his enormous trunk.

- Two women from the Middle East. They are wearing long black robes and their heads and faces are covered.

- Three women struggling to carry a long, rolled-up carpet.

- A group of teenagers wearing school jackets.

- Two elderly people wearing huge coats and hats. The man and woman are both stooped and walking with the help of canes.

No other people board the ship, so you feel certain that the short, thin man has not appeared. You are the last one to climb the gangplank. The boat whistle sounds, and the ship leaves the harbor. You feel a bit disappointed that you haven't been able to help the police find the escaped prisoner.

Then, suddenly, when the boat is midway across Lake Michigan, you see a short, thin man near one of the state rooms. He is on board.

If you were writing an explanation for how this baffling scenario happened, how would you explain the way the man boarded without being seen? Use only realistic ideas. He can't be invisible, for instance, and he can't have help from miraculous inventions or alien machines. Your ideas will show that kids can, indeed, be extremely observant and clever.

After you've finished, compare your solution with the thoughts that other young detectives have had.

Possible Solutions

1. The man might have hidden himself in the cargo.
   a. Perhaps he was hiding in the back seat of one of the cars that the crew members drove aboard.
   b. Perhaps he was concealed in one of the large boxes or barrels.
   c. Perhaps he was in the carpet that the three women carried.
   d. Perhaps he was in the trunk that the tall man brought on board.
2. The man might have boarded the boat in an unusual manner.
   a. Perhaps he sneaked on board before the regular boarding process.
   b. Perhaps he used ropes to climb up the side while everyone was busy watching the cargo being loaded.
   c. Perhaps he used scuba gear and clung to the side of the ship until it was well out into the water. Then he used ropes to climb up unobserved.
3. He might have disguised himself. He could have pretended to be . . .
   a. a crewman. He could have stolen a uniform and joined the others.
   b. the plump passenger. He could have used padding to make himself look heavier.
   c. either one of the black-robed women or one of the three women who were carrying the carpet. A wig and women's clothing would be a good disguise.
   d. either one of the old people. He could have slumped and limped deliberately.
   e. a teenager. He could have joined the throng of teens, dressed exactly the way they were dressed.

Were you able to think of any other possibilities? By using this type of imagining, mystery writers concoct puzzling plots for stories. And often a youth sleuth is the only character in the book who sees the clues to the solution because kids have such great imaginations!

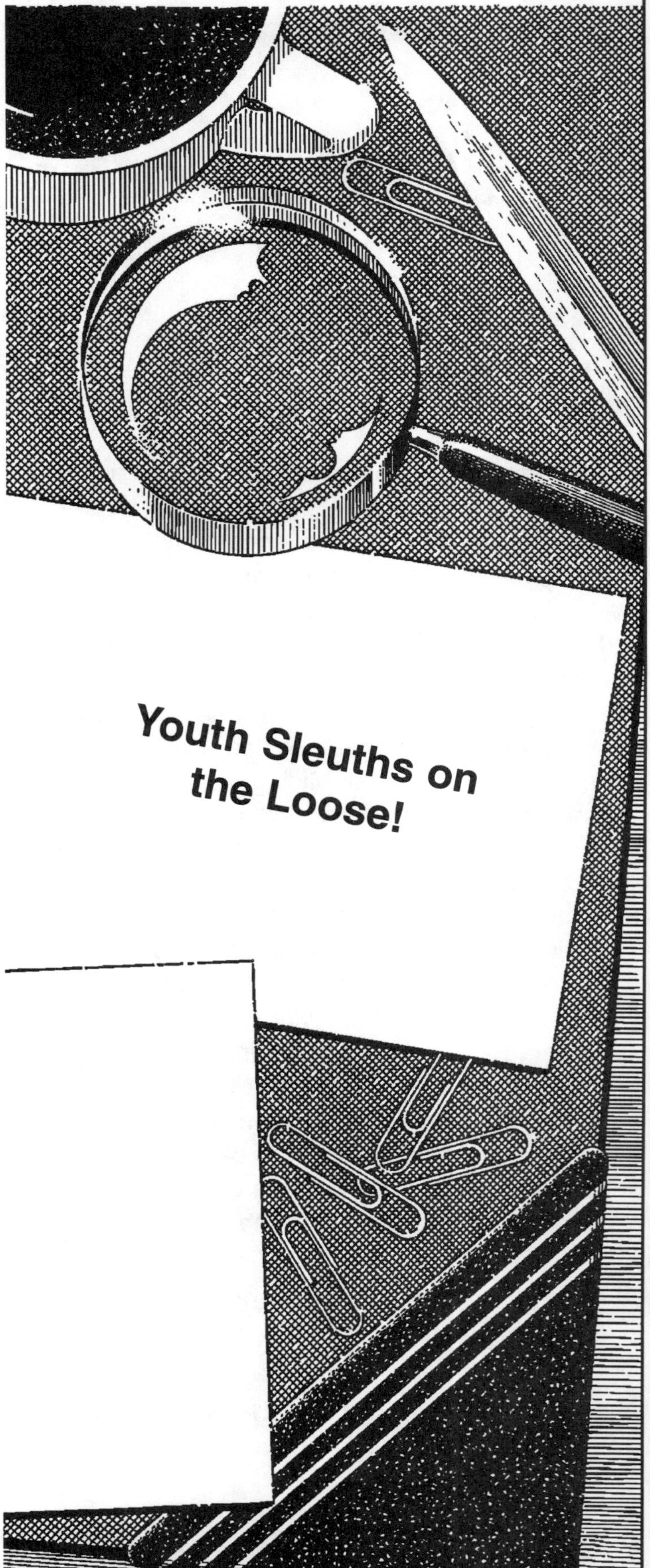

Can You Solve This?

Math Games to Make You Think

So what does the message say?

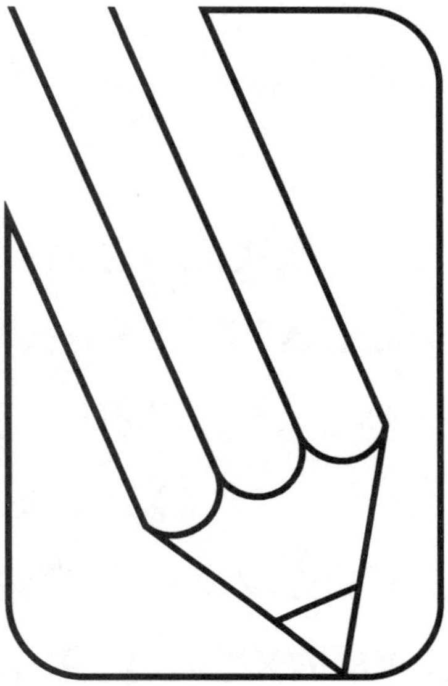

Curricular fit: data management, problem solving, and language development

Special features: The activity integrates reading, language development, and data management in the context of a real-world situation—data encoding and decoding. Data encoding and decoding is a normal part of what happens in the real world. The Central Intelligence Agency (CIA) does it, big business does it, cable TV does it, and so on.

A > E
B > F
C > G
D > H
E > I
.
.
.
W > A
X > B
Y > C
Z > D

There are many ways to encode messages. Most real-world data encoding and decoding systems involve quite complex mathematics (such as the prime factorization of huge composite numbers). There are some simple ways to encode messages that are appropriate for primary and middle school students. One appropriate way is to shift the letters of the alphabet.

Suppose that all the letters of the alphabet are shifted up by five positions. The encoding scheme would be like what is shown to the left. If this encoding scheme is used to encode the word *BAD*, the encoded word would be *FEH*. To decode *FEH*, one just thinks in reverse (F -> B, E -> A, and H -> D).

You (or a small group of students) can decide on an encoding scheme that involves shifting the alphabet. Encode a long message using that scheme. On page 12, there is a sample secret message consisting of two problems. Both problems are encoded using the scheme described above. The spaces between words have been removed to make the decoding task more difficult (and that should make a data-management approach to decoding the message more appealing). Also this is more in line with the way real-world data encoding works. Sentences have been left intact. The answer to the first problem is "It all depends on how the cats cooperate to catch the rats." The answer to the second problem is "You need to pull out exactly three socks to get a matching pair." The sentences have been decoded on the next page.

PROBLEM 1

MJXLVIIGEXWGEXGLXLVIIVEXWMRXLVII
QMRYXIW,LSAQERCGEXWAMPPGEXGLSRI
LYRHVIHVEXWMRSRILYRHVIHQMRYXIW?

PROBLEM 2

XIRVIHWSGOWERHXIRFPYIWSGOWEVIEP
PQMBIHYTMRSRIHVIWWIVHVEAIV.XLI
XAIRXCWSGOWEVIIBEGXPCEPMOIIBGITXJSV
XLIMVGSPSV.XLIVSSQMWMRTMXGL
HEVORIWWERHCSYAERXQEXGLMRKWSGOW.
ALEXMWXLIWQEPPIWXRYQFIVSJWSGOWCSY
QYWXXEOISYXSJXLIHVEAIVMRSVHIVXSFI
GIVXEMRXLEXCSYKIXEQEXGLMRKTEMV?

KSSH KSMRK. CSY HMH MX.

Alphabet Frequency Table

Letter	Occurrence
A	8/100 = .08
B	2/100 = .02
C	4/100 = .04
D	4/100 = .04
E	13/100 = .13
F	2/100 = .02
G	2/100 = .02
H	6/100 = .06
I	8/100 = .08
J	1/100 = .01
K	1/100 = .01
L	4/100 = .04
M	4/100 = .04
N	8/100 = .08
O	8/100 = .08
P	2/100 = .02
Q	5/1000 = .005
R	8/100 = .08
S	8/100 = .08
T	10/100 = .10
U	4/100 = .04
V	2/100 = .02
W	2/100 = .02
X	1/100 = .01
Y	2/100 = .02
Z	7/1000 = .007

Have students decode the message. Most students will try letter substitutions in a random way. After a time, suggest that a clue to finding out the secret message can be found by reading a Sherlock Holmes mystery (*The Adventure of the Dancing Men* by Sir Arthur Conan Doyle). By reading the story, students should realize that if they find the letter that appears the most often in the secret message, then they will most likely have found the letter that is matched with E. If necessary, provide the further hint that each letter is matched with one of the letters of the alphabet in the same way.

Many follow-up activities are possible. Here is one example. Have students examine a variety of reading materials such as newspapers, magazines, and school textbooks. The project could involve obtaining an estimate of the frequency of occurrence of each letter of the alphabet. This estimate could then be compared to estimates from other reading materials.

You might find the alphabet frequency table on page 12 useful at some point in relation to the activity. Note that the percentages of occurrences of each letter do not total 100. This is often the case when probability values are obtained from real-world empirical data.

Problem 1:
If three cats catch three rats in three minutes, how many cats will catch one hundred rats in one hundred minutes?

Problem 2:
Ten red socks and ten blue socks are all mixed up in one dresser drawer. The twenty socks are exactly alike except for their color. The room is in pitch darkness and you want matching socks. What is the smallest number of socks you must take out of the drawer in order to be certain that you get a matching pair?
Good going. You did it.

Sharing, and sharing, and sharing . . .

Suggested grade level: grade 4 to 5

Curricular fit: multiplication, multiples of three, meaning of division and remainders, and problem solving

Special features: The activity involves solving an interesting problem. It could be part of a unit on multiplication or preliminary division (understanding the division symbol is not required for the activity).

Present the granola bar problem on page 14 in the context of a thematic unit as an interesting homework assignment. The problem is likely to get the adults at home involved in solving it. To solve the problem, have students use concrete objects to represent the granola bars. Trial and error will be the most suitable strategy along with some thinking about multiples of 3. Once the problem is solved by using concrete materials, have students represent the solution symbolically by showing each step (each splitting up of the pile) in the form of a multiplication number sentence (79 = 3 x 26 + 1; 52 = 3 x 17 + 1; 34 = 3 x 11 + 1; 22 = 3 x 7 + 1). Representing the solution symbolically engages the students in more abstract thinking and makes it possible to see a numerical pattern (the starting number in the pile for the next step is double the share that was removed in the step before, and these doubles must be one larger than a multiple of 3). Note that symbolically representing each step by division is not necessary for solving the problem.

Good luck with the granola bar problem! (The least number of granola bars to satisfy the conditions of the story is 79 bars.)

Granola Bar Problem

Three children, Zach, Bailey, and Devin, and their pet Vietnamese pot-bellied pig are snowbound in a cabin in the mountains. They decide to put all of their granola bars into one pile. They each contribute whatever granola bars they have to the pile. They are going to share the bars equally in the morning (the pig doesn't get any). They are sleepy from all of the work and go to bed.

During the night, Zach wakes up to go to the bathroom. Everyone else is sleeping. He decides to take his share now. So he splits the pile into three equal groups and takes his share. Unfortunately, there is one extra bar left over in the pile. Feeling generous, he gives it to the pig, who eats it right away. Then he puts the two other groups together to make a new pile.

Bailey also wakes up during the night after having a nightmare. Everyone else is sleeping. She decides to take her share now. So she splits the pile into three equal groups and takes her share. She also finds that there is one extra bar left in the pile. Feeling generous, she gives it to the pig, who eats it right away. Then she puts the two other groups together to make a new pile.

Devin wakes up just before morning. He is an early bird. Everyone else is sleeping. He decides to take his share now. So he splits the pile into three equal groups and takes his share. Once again, there is one extra bar left over in the pile. Feeling generous, he gives it to the pig, who eats it right away. Then he puts the two other groups together to make a new pile.

When everyone wakes up, each of them, of course, notices that the pile is smaller than it was the evening before. No one says anything, as each of them has something to hide and the pig can't talk. They split the pile into three equal groups. Again, there is one granola bar left over. They give it to the pig and each of them takes an equal share. All of them are smiling.

What is the smallest number of granola bars that could have been in the pile in the evening so that it all works out as described in the story?

The Robbery at the Chromatography Bank

Police Dept. Official File

Frontal/Front View Only		Profile/Side View Only	
Suspect Name: Rocky Cleaver	Age: 38	Height: 6' 1"	Weight: 190
Occupation: Delivery man	Eyes: brown	Hobby: Watches television	Hair: black

Goals

1. Exposure to lab procedures
2. Exposure to chromatography, chemistry
3. Convergent thinking
4. Adding challenge and pizazz to learning

This Activity Provides

1. Fluency (search, identify)
2. Flexibility (categorize, interpret, contrast)
3. Originality (construct, illustrate)
4. Complexity (solve)
5. Curiosity (inquire)

Materials

- 5 different brands of pretested water-based black felt-tip or roller-ball marking pens
- scissors
- paper cups
- pencils—six per student or team
- water container
- water
- 6 pieces white paper towel
- 5 mug shots
- Scotch™ tape
- 6 notes
- 8 1/2" x 11" white paper

Chromatography

This exercise exposes students to the science of chromatography, and, by using this method, they can identify a bank robber from a group of suspects. Chemists use chromatography as a tool to separate substances and to discover what substances make up a mixture. Substances migrate through an absorbent material at different rates, and this experiment shows this process in a colorful and exciting way. The actual colors in black water-based ink will surprise the students as the colors separate while being pulled through the paper towels. In many ink formulas four, five, or six colors (pigments) will appear as the process proceeds.

Setup

An attempted robbery has just occurred at the Chromatography Bank. The unsuccessful attempt ended when five suspects were trapped inside the lobby of the bank. The problem the authorities face is that the discarded gloves, disguise, and a bag of money were found on the lobby floor, and the bank teller cannot identify the thief because he or she saw only the disguise and not the person.

The robber left this note lying on the counter:

> Please deposit the cash in the bag.
> S.W.A.K.
> The Robber

Each suspect agreed to be searched and notes were found on each of them. Descriptions of notes can be found on page 19. Descriptions of suspects can be found throughout this activity.

Note Preparation

Each note is written with a different pen, but one will match the robber's note. This can change from class to class so that the perpetrator changes for each group.

Be sure a bold outline is written around each note (with the same pen) for the chromatography test! The notes are written on paper towels.

The Task

1. Introduce the setup. Introduce the suspects via mug shots.
2. Divide the class into groups of three to four.
3. Distribute supplies (not the notes yet).
4. Demonstrate paper chromatography process (page 17).
5. Each group performs a chromatography test on a strip from the robbery note.
6. Observe color separation beginning.
7. Each group performs chromatography tests on strips from all five suspects' notes.
8. After 10–15 minutes, pull all test strips and tape them to the same sheet of 8 1/2" x 11" white paper.
9. Have each group state who it believes to be the robber based on the chromatography results.

Police Dept. Official File

Frontal/Front View Only		Profile/Side View Only	
Suspect Name: Reggie Chattsworth III	Age: 47	Height: 5' 10 1/2"	Weight: 190
Occupation: Spy	Eyes: blue	Hobby: Codes and Cyphers	Hair: brown

Chromatography Process

1. Cut strips from notes.

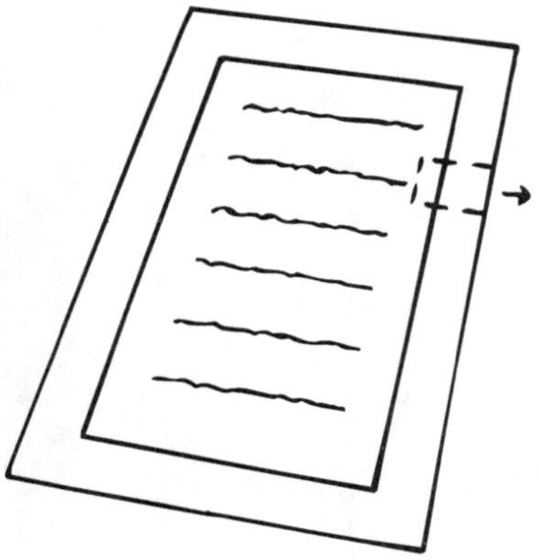

2. Tape note to pencil.

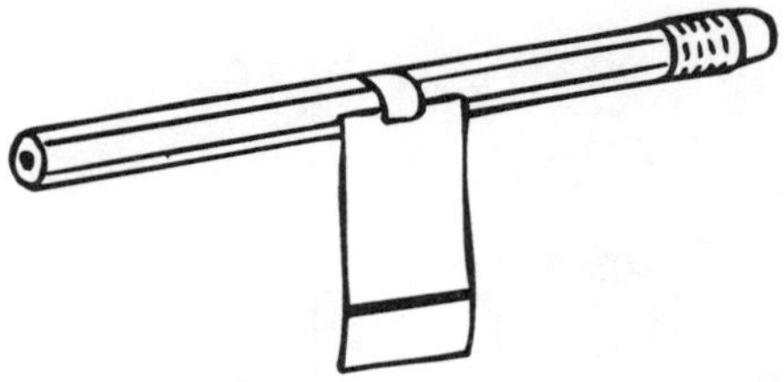

3. Pour water into cup (no spills) so that the test strip will barely touch the water.

4. Lay pencil on cup with the note (test strip) just touching the water. Do not allow the water to touch the ink.

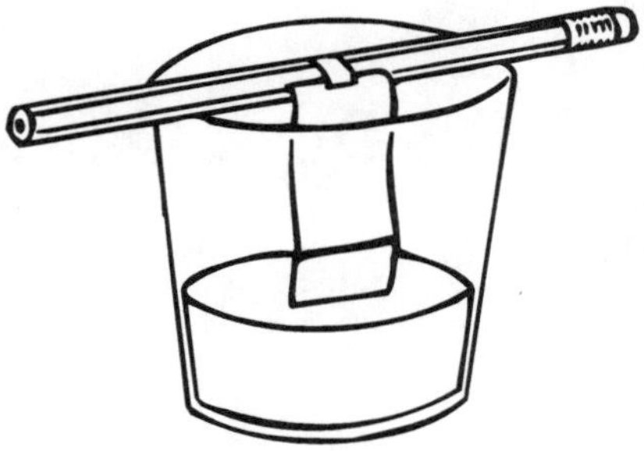

5. Repeat procedure with the other test strips.

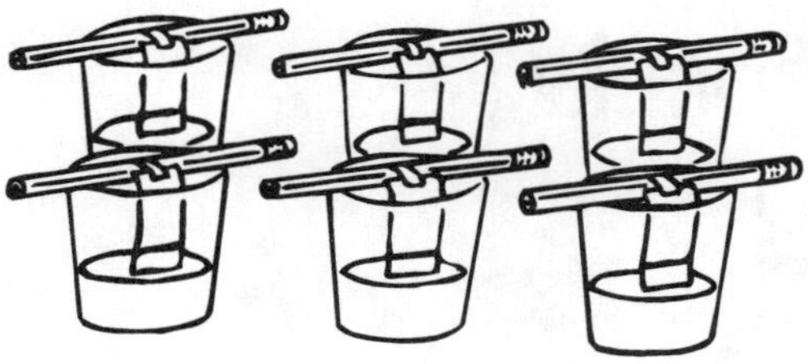

6. Remove, dry, mount, compare, present results to group.

Suggestions

1. An interesting and challenging variation is to use two different bank notes, each matching a different suspect. Challenge the groups to attempt to solve these apparently confusing results and see how long it takes them to realize that the two suspects were both in on the bungled heist.
2. Suggest neatness and good organization at the start.
3. The students will have to realize that they need to create some method to identify the smears so they can be differentiated from one another. You may choose whether or not to warn them about this.

Police Dept. Official File

Frontal/Front View Only
Suspect Name: Joyce Ann Perrin Age: 29
Occupation: Homemaker, mom Eyes: blue

Profile/Side View Only
Height: 5' 8" Weight: 128
Hobby: P.T.A. and fishing Hair: brown

Police Dept. Official File

Frontal/Front View Only
Suspect Name: Vinnie Tiddley Age: 13
Occupation: Student Eyes: brown

Profile/Side View Only
Height: 5' 1" Weight: 80
Hobby: Making faces Hair: black

Police Dept. Official File

Frontal/Front View Only
Suspect Name: Mavis Smootyer (Granny) Age: 89
Occupation: Computer repair Eyes: blue

Profile/Side View Only
Height: 4' 10" Weight: 246
Hobby: Model trains Hair: gray

Police Dept. Official File

Frontal/Front View Only
Suspect Name: I. C. Yootoo Age: 27
Occupation: Rock star Eyes: hazel

Profile/Side View Only
Height: 6' 0" Weight: 167
Hobby: Knitting Hair: blue

Robbery Note

Reggie's Note

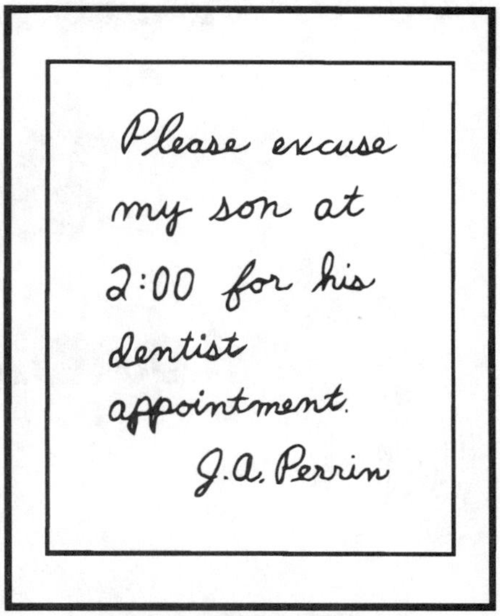

J.A. Perrin's Note

Mavis' Note

Vinnie T.'s Note

I.C. Yootoo's Note

Rocky C.'s Note

Whodunnit?

An Outline for a Mystery/Detective Unit

A mystery/detective unit is a great opportunity for students to apply their deductive logic and reasoning skills. In this particular unit, students work together and independently, choosing projects which suit their individual learning styles. The unit also incorporates elements of problem solving, planning, creative writing, and dramatic production.

Objectives: During the course of this unit, students will . . .

1. Use deductive logic, sequencing, and reasoning skills to solve group mysteries.
2. Learn to discern between facts and inferences.
3. Find elements of a mystery in newspaper stories.
4. Use research skills to investigate famous mystery authors and their detective characters.
5. Work in a small group to create an original mystery skit and present it for classmates to solve.
6. Complete an independent creative project based on a mystery book of their choice.
7. Come dressed as a character from their book to present their independent projects to an audience of classmates.

General Daily Outline

Day 1

- Students see how many words they can make using the letters in MYSTERIOUS.
- Students work together as a group to try to solve a mystery from mixed-up clue cards. These are available from several places, or you can create your own. One good source for these cards is *Mysteries for Group Detectives* by Betty Jett and Peggy Grossmann (Synergetics).

Day 2

- Students choose a mystery book to read on their own during the unit. Project options are discussed (see page 22). The projects will be presented by students who are dressed as characters from their books on Day 14 of the unit.
- After discussing the importance of determining the sequence of events in solving a crime, two teams of students compete in putting mixed-up events in the correct chronological order to solve a mystery. Here again, the clue cards from *Mysteries for Group Detectives* can be used, or you can create your own.

Day 3

- Presented with several magazine pictures, students list everything they know for certain (facts) and everything they can logically deduce (inferences) from what they see. It's fun to use some tricky pictures here in order to show them the hazard of jumping to conclusions.

- Students attempt to solve an Encyclopedia Brown case which is read aloud to them by the teacher or by another student, paying careful attention to their use of both facts and inferences.

Day 4

- Students list and discuss the elements of a mystery, such as the characters (victim, criminal, suspects, witnesses, investigator), setting, crime, motive, sequence of events, clues, evidence, and solution.

- Students find examples of these elements in newspaper clippings which describe real-life mysteries being currently solved by the police. You may want to provide certain newspaper pages or sections which you know contain examples appropriate for the students to read and discuss.

Day 5

- Rent a video of a Sherlock Holmes story, such as "The Red-Headed League." Stop it before Sherlock Holmes actually solves the case. Have the students work with partners to try to solve it themselves, based on what they've seen so far. After hearing everyone's solution, finish playing the video and discuss the results.

Day 6

- On page 22 is a list of famous mystery authors and their famous detective characters. As students arrive, place either the name of a famous mystery author or the name of that author's famous detective character on each student's back. Students must ask each other questions about their identities and use reference and resource materials to determine both who they themselves are and who they should be matched with (for example, Sir Arthur Conan Doyle would be matched with Sherlock Holmes). The paired-up partners then tell the class what they've learned about who they are.

Days 7, 8, and 9

- Students break into groups of five or six students. During the next three days, they will create their own mystery skit with all the elements previously discussed. They must first decide on a crime. (You may want to limit them to nonviolent crimes such as counterfeiting, embezzling, burglary, larceny, and so on.) Then have them write an opening scene which shows the discovery of the crime by the victim. They must then introduce three suspects, each of whom has a motive as well as an alibi. One of them is the criminal. The audience's job will be to use the clues and evidence presented to determine which of the three suspects is really the criminal. The audience will also have the opportunity to ask questions of the victim, witness, and suspects. After they've reached their decision, the closing scene will be presented, showing how the crime actually took place, thereby revealing whether or not the audience solved the case correctly.

- Separate work areas may be needed in order to maintain secrecy since each group will be the other group's audience.

Days 9,10 and 11

- Students rehearse their skits, plan props and costumes, and make any scenery or signs they plan to use to enhance their presentation.

Days 12 and 13

- One group presents its mystery skit for the other group, which acts as an audience trying to solve the mystery through questions and clues. The following day they switch, and the other group presents its skit while the first group acts as the audience. You may want to videotape the presentations and let the students watch themselves on the final day.

Day 14

- Students come dressed as a character in the mystery book they chose to read during the unit. They present their projects to the class, giving a little background information about the book. The projects are then displayed in the classroom or library.

Day 15

- Students watch the videotape of their mystery skits, if available. Students play mystery board games or computer games such as Clue, Solve It! (Sunburst Software) or Snooper Troops (Broderbund).

Mystery Book Project Options

1. Build a 3-D map/model of the story's setting. Show important places where significant events take place. Label all places.

2. Write a mini-diary from a character's point of view. Include at least six entries, describing events, thoughts, feelings, and suspicions.

3. Illustrate five significant events from the story. Make them colorful and at least 81/2" x 11" in size. Bind them together in a booklet.

4. Create a museum box display by collecting 10 items that played an important role in the story. Arrange the items in a large, clear-covered, flat box. Label each item, telling its significance.

5. Write a different ending to the story. Begin with a summary of what has happened so far. Then write your new ending using descriptive narration and interactive dialogue. Your final copy should be written clearly on nice paper.

6. Tape-record a dramatization of an important scene from the story. Use sound effects and clear speaking voices to set the mood of the scene. Introduce the scene and the actors at the beginning of your recording.

Famous Mystery Authors and Their Detective Characters

Sir Arthur Conan Doyle–Sherlock Holmes

Carolyn Keene–Nancy Drew

Frank Dixon–Hardy Boys

Donald J. Sobol–Encyclopedia Brown

G.K. Chesterton–Father Brown

Rex Stout–Nero Wolfe

Edgar Allan Poe–C. Auguste Dupin

Raymond Chandler–Philip Marlowe

A Bushel of Apples

Encounter With Apples

Select a group of five children to lead the encounter.

For Encounter 1, give each child a different variety of apple to hold. Have them imagine they **are** that apple.

For Encounter 2, give each child a different form of apple to hold: jar of applesauce; dried apple slice; carton of apple cider or juice; restaurant package of apple jelly; caramel apple; or a piece of apple-flavored candy. Have them imagine they **are** that item.

Encounter 1

1. Describe how your appearance is similar to and different from the other apples.
2. Explain your feelings (good/bad) about being an apple.
3. What would you add to yourself, or take away, that would make you more desirable?
4. Someone is just about to take a bite out of you. What would you say if you could suddenly talk?
5. What makes you so special in a basket of fruit?

Encounter 2

1. What is your relationship to a fresh apple?
2. Explain why you feel luckier or not as lucky as a fresh apple.
3. If you could change one thing about yourself, what would it be?
4. If apples could no longer be grown or sold in America, how would it affect you?
5. What is your greatest asset or advantage to the consumer?

Follow up with selected task-card activities.

Scamper With Apples!

S: substitute

C: combine

A: adapt; adopt

M: modify; minimize; magnify

P: put to another use

E: elaborate; eliminate

R: reverse; rearrange

S: Your teacher is allergic to apples. How else could she use the one you brought her today?

C: Certain foods just seem to go together (Examples: peaches and cream, ice cream and cookies). What would make an ideal "apple and . . ." combination?

A: What processes do we use to preserve apples so we can eat them when they are not in season?

M: Apple seeds are very small. Many people even eat the core! How would the way we prepare apples change if they had a seed like a peach pit?

P: What are all the ways an apple tree can be used? Think of uses other than by people!

E: What are all the expressions you can think of that include the word *apple* (Example: "apple of my eye")? Or, take the apple out of the story "Snow White and the Seven Dwarfs." How would the events change?

R: What if apples grew underground instead of on trees? What would be affected by this difference?

Whole-Class Apple Adventure

Bring in a bag or bushel basket of apples. Try to have as many different varieties as possible and at least one or two apples per child. Make a grid chart to use, compiling your observation data and filling it in as you go along!

This is a great activity for parent involvement, small groups, or team assignments. Photograph or videotape it and donate it to the library.

1. Talk about the observable characteristics of apples.
   Shape: round, squat, long, with or without shoulders
   Skin: color, texture, solid, stripes, "freckles"
2. Cut one of each apple variety in half horizontally. Examine the exposed seed core for: seed pattern, seed shape, number of seeds.
3. Assess each apple variety for the following factors:
   Inside color: snow white, cream white, greenish white
   Texture: crispy, juicy, mushy, dry
   Taste: sweet, tart, mouth-puckery
4. Have each child weigh an apple or assign an apple to each team of three or four. Search for objects that are about the same size but
   - weigh more
   - weigh less
   - weigh about the same
5. Bring in a chip basket, a peck basket, and a bushel basket. What is the difference in size, shape, and weight? How are apples sold? by number? size? weight?
6. Conduct a taste test of the different varieties. Make a picture graph of student preferences (for lower grades) or give "awards" for sweetest, juiciest, tartest, and so on.
7. Dry some apple slices. Make applesauce and freeze some. Sometime later in the year, eat your apple treats.

Activities

(Place these on apple-shaped task cards.)

1. Make a list of all the words you can make from the letters in APPLESAUCE.

2. Make a list of all the words that describe how an apple tastes. Use your list to create a poem.

3. Make a list of all the words that describe sounds you associate with eating a crispy, juicy apple. Use your list to create a poem.

4. Specifically describe an apple to a person who cannot see.

5. Students often bring apples to their teachers. Make a list of all possible reasons for doing this. Do you have some better "treat" ideas?

6. Use one of the large task-card shapes to write a book with the title: *I Am the Apple of My Mother's Eye When . . . .*

7. An old saying goes: "An apple a day keeps the doctor away." Make up a collection of sayings that begin with "An apple a day . . . ."

8. Make a collection of five-word sentences whose words begin with the letters in *apple.* Example:
   All **P**ink **P**anthers **L**ove **E**nchiladas!

9. Survey your classmates to find out how they best like to eat apples. Do they prefer a fresh apple? applesauce? apple cider? apple butter? dried apple slices? caramel apples? Graph your findings.

10. Mothers are always looking for new and healthful snack combinations for their kids! How many ways can you think of to "dress up" apples? Example: Apple wedges with peanut butter.

11. Research the processes used to make apple products. Use cookbooks as reference material. Write up one as a flow chart or computer program. Consider: cider, jelly, applesauce, apple pie.

12. What is the average number of seeds in an apple? On a day the whole class has an apple for snack, have everyone count the seeds in their apple cores. Then average. Try it again another time and compare.

13. Johnny Appleseed's birthday is September 26. Use an apple design to create the ideal birthday party—complete with menu, favors, wrapping-paper design, and possible gift ideas.

14. Read a story about Johnny Appleseed's life. Create an interview with Johnny Appleseed, answering the questions based on facts you learned from your reading.

15. Johnny Appleseed is considered a folk hero. What are the characteristics of folk heroes? How did Johnny Appleseed exhibit these characteristics?

16. Apples are used for temptation in some fairy tales—Snow White was tricked by a poisoned apple! Change your favorite fairy tale to include the use of an apple to tempt the main character.

17. Use the different types of apples as characters in a story or play. Characters: "Dee Licious," "Granny Smith," "Mac Intosh," "Jonathan," "The Rome Beauty," and "The Wine Sap."

18. Collect pictures of words that have a short *a* vowel sound. Collect pictures of words that begin with short *a.* Make an apple story using as many of your pictures as you can.

19. Research how the different types of apples got their names. What are their characteristics and best uses? Chart your information.

20. Apples can no longer be considered safe for eating! Make a list of all the ways apples could be used instead of as a food source.

21. You are the worm who lives in an apple. Defend your right to live there, describing all the ways the apple is important to you.

22. You are one apple in a whole bushel basket. Everyone sees you as just another apple, but you know you're special. Explain all the things that set you apart from the others.

23. You are an apple tree. You have been asked to be a guest speaker for a classroom. Make a list of 10–15 questions you might be asked and tell how you would answer.

24. Make a picture chart of the effect each season has on an apple tree. What does each season contribute to the development of an apple?

For Upper Grade Levels

25. A neighbor has decided to plant an apple orchard on land that adjoins yours. List the ways his decisions will be a benefit or detriment to your way of life. How might it affect your grandchildren in 40 years?

26. Draw a diagram that illustrates the life cycle of an apple from seed to tree to blossom to apple to seed. Illustrate the possible factors at each stage that could interfere with, or prevent, the continuing life process.

27. Acid rain, pollution, and insecticides will destroy fruit orchards around the world within the next 25 years. What options might scientists consider to assure that future generations will enjoy apples? Rank the options by practicality.

28. Aquaculture is a new science that is looking to the ocean as a possible source of "farmland" for the future. Design a complex that would allow apple orchards to be grown on the ocean floor. What problems must be anticipated?

Ant-ivities

1.

Many ants live in tunnels in the ground. These tunnels include rooms for various activities.

Draw a diagram of a highly developed underground ant hill. Label your diagram to explain the various points of interest.

2.

Suppose a couple of very observant ants came into our classroom one day.

Write the conversation that would go on between them.

Make some ant puppets and present a play.

3.

When an ant nest is disturbed, the workers rush around protecting the queen and moving the eggs and babies to a safer location.

Write a diary entry of an ant who had this sort of experience. Be sure to get across the feeling of panic and terror that would result.

4.

Pretend you are the leader of some worker ants.

Draw a map of a picnic area and then plan an attack on a picnic. Make a list of your instructions, referring to the map where possible.

5.

Draw pictures to show what the following would look like if they were in the ANT world:

ANTarctica
pANTher
cANTeen
phANTom
giANT
pANTs
cANTankerous
ANTi-gravity
lANTern
fANTasyland
Add your own ideas.

6.

What sorts of things might ants have needed in the old days?

Make a museum display of old ANTiques.

7.

Some ants build huge castles, or hills.

Design an ant castle to protect the queen. Show where she would be kept, deep within the castle.

Explain what the various defenses would be for, and how they would work.

8.

Anteaters love to eat ants. Make a cookbook for anteaters. Make your recipes as creative as possible.

9.

Often ants make pests of themselves by getting into houses.

Make a floor plan of your kitchen at home and draw a dotted line to show the trail the ants would follow to get to all the goodies. Be sure to label your plan.

10.

Ants cannot talk, but they can communicate very well. For example, they can tell one another where they found food or that the nest has been attacked.

Pretend you are a scientist who has learned how the ants communicate. Write a “dictionary” that shows how to translate ant language into English.

11.

Some ants allow other small insects such as crickets or tiny cockroaches to live with them.

You are the ant owner of an ant hotel. Make a sign listing rules for such “guests” staying at your place.

12.

Ants spend a lot of time cleaning and grooming themselves.

Make a list of beauty products for an ant. Use these ideas to design an advertisement for an ant magazine.

13.

Some ants capture other smaller ants and keep them for slaves.

One ant was recently captured, but it managed to escape. Be an ant reporter and write a newspaper article to tell the tale. A "photo" and headline would add a lot to your story.

14.

Some ants cut leaves into little pieces to take back to their nests.

Be an ant artist. Tear construction paper into little pieces and make a mosaic picture using these pieces. Give it an ANTeresting title.

15.

Ants often boss around little green insects called aphids. They herd them much the same way that cowboys herd cattle. Ants like to "milk" the aphids for the sweet juice they make from flowers.

Draw a picture of some "cowboy ants," and write a description of what is going on.

16.

Imagine you are the General of the Army Ants.

Create a training manual for teaching your ant recruits what to do.

17.

List 10 ways in which an Army Ant might be adapted for fighting.

Draw a picture of what it might look like. Then design armor and weaponry for it.

18.

Plan your own ant activity here.

Let's Celebrate! Time

Come On—Join In!

What is a celebration? This unit will allow students to think about celebrations and analyze them to discover why we have them, who participates in them, and how they differ from one another yet are similar. These activities also allow students to show their own creativity.

Question Answering

1. Make a list of days we celebrate.
2. Make a list of things we celebrate.
3. Make a list of ways we celebrate.
4. What is the difference between a celebration and a holiday?
5. What is the difference between a celebration and a party?
6. Make a list of three days we celebrate in the United States, and match the days up with colors that we would use if we were having a public celebration.
7. Make a list of people whose careers are dependent upon celebrations.
8. Make a list of people whose careers may be affected by celebrations and tell how.
9. What day do you think is personally celebrated more than any other day? Why?
10. Choose a country and research a day celebrated there that is not celebrated in the United States.
11. What is the difference between a religious holiday and a national holiday?
12. Make a list of days that are celebrated that are not listed on a calendar.

13. Why would one country's calendar of holidays differ from our calendar?

14. Make a list of special people, real or imaginary, who are associated with holidays, and match them up with the holiday to which they are connected.

15. How does a day become a national holiday?

16. Make a list of items that may be connected with any celebration.

17. Make a list of symbols that are connected with particular holidays, and match them up with the holiday.

18. List all the holidays that we celebrate on a particular day, regardless of where it falls on the calendar.

19. List all the days we celebrate that may change according to the calendar.

Creating

Make up a new reason to celebrate! Thinking about the following things will help to create your celebration.

1. What is the reason for the new celebration?

2. Who will be participating in this celebration?

3. What is the primary activity or activities involved?

4. When will this celebration take place?

5. Where will this celebration take place?

6. Choose some colors that you want to represent this celebration.

7. Make a card for someone who would appreciate this type of celebration.

8. Choose a symbol for this celebration and show it the way you would want it displayed.

9. Create some products that one may purchase if one wanted to get involved in this celebration.

Critical Thinking

1. Choose two celebrations. On a Venn diagram, show how they are similar and how they are different.

2. Do a mind mapping of your favorite holiday.

3. Choose two holidays and debate why one is better than the other.

4. Debate the issue: People do/do not need to celebrate.

5. Compare the benefits and the flaws of celebrations.

6. List all the ways you would know what holiday was being celebrated without knowing the particular day.

7. Debate the issue: Holidays should/should not be celebrated according to convenience, but on the day they fall on the calendar.

8. Explain how one's culture will affect the way he or she celebrates.

9. Make a sequence chart of how a holiday becomes a national holiday.

10. Explain the difference between a national day of celebration and a legal holiday. Give examples of each.

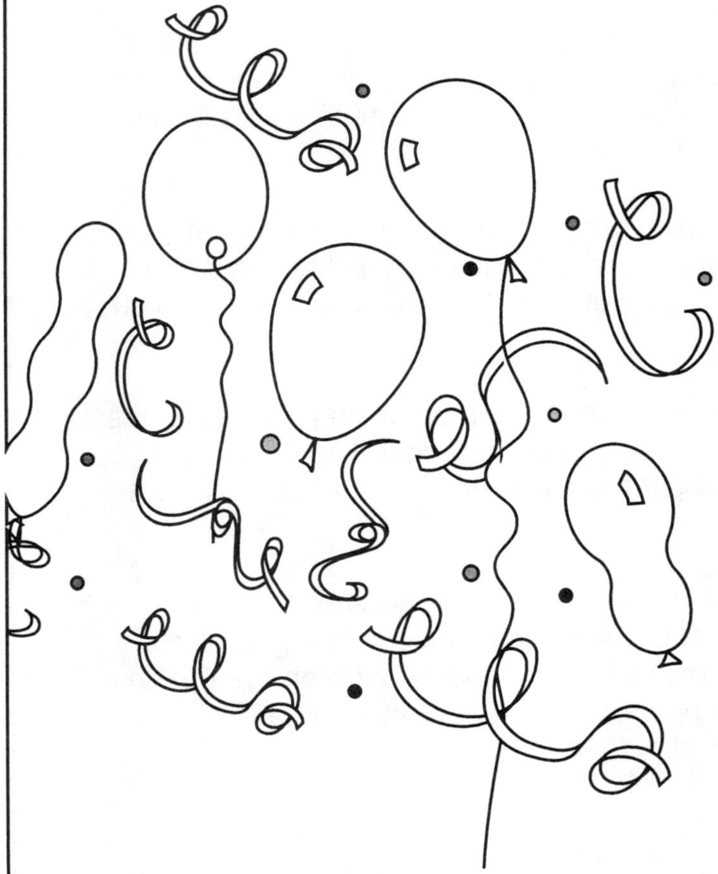

Encounter Lesson

Become a symbol for a particular holiday. What symbol are you? Describe yourself in specific detail. How do you feel about being this symbol? Tell how you are used. Describe a person that might use you. Tell how you feel about being used. Tell how you feel in regard to this particular person. What ultimately happens to you at the end of the holiday? Tell how you feel about this.

Creative and Critical Thinking

1. Create a crossword puzzle of celebrations.

2. Create a game with celebrations as the focus.

3. Design a quilt of holidays/celebrations for a couple that just married. Show how that quilt might change after they have been married for 50 years.

4. Analyzing a person's life span, what celebrations would that person participate in outside of holidays?

5. If you were a storeowner, what product would you believe would make the most money as far as celebrations go? Analyze the cost and the profit.

6. Tell or show how a calendar might stay similar as far as celebrations/holidays go for three years, but on the fourth year it becomes much more involved.

7. Make a new song by changing the symbols of a holiday song to fit the symbols of another holiday.

SCAMPER

Substitute—Put the character from one holiday in a story involving another holiday. Write your own story. What would Santa do on the Fourth of July? What would the Easter Bunny do at Halloween?

Combine—Combine symbols of different holidays and what do you get? What would you do with egg lights, Halloween baskets, or Fourth of July cornucopias?

Adapt—What would happen if you had no money for Christmas presents? What could you give instead? What would happen if the costume you planned to wear to a Halloween party was too small for you to wear and there was no time to go buy another one? What would you do if you misplaced the grass you were going to put in the bottom of your spring basket and you needed the basket now?

Modify, Magnify, or Minify—What would you do if all hens started laying eggs the size of basketballs right before the big holiday? How would it affect sales, and how would you dye the eggs? What could you do if the Easter Bunny was the size of Big Foot? What could you do if the only baskets available were the size of a teacup?

Put to Other Uses—What would happen if a store had too many witch costumes after Halloween, too much wrapping paper after Christmas, or too many firecrackers after the Fourth of July? Pick a holiday and tell how you would get rid of the excess inventory if you were the storeowner.

Eliminate—What would you do if the firecracker companies went on strike right before the Fourth of July? What would you do if there were no dye for eggs? What would you do if you ran out of wrapping paper and you have to give a gift tomorrow and it's too late to go to the store?

Reverse, Rearrange—You have just been given notice that you will be spending the holidays on the opposite side of the world. This means that the climate is totally different. How is this going to affect your celebration? For example, it's 3° below zero on the Fourth of July or 100° in the shade on Thanksgiving. What changes will you make in regard to your celebrations?

The Colors of My World

1. Brainstorm a list of phrases that have to do with color. Break down the lists according to specific colors to determine which color has the most phrases connected with it.

2. Choose a spot in the world that you think most represents a specific season. Where would you find spring colors the majority of the time? How about winter, summer, and fall colors? Then use an atlas to give the map coordinates of your season.

3. Use the atlas to find places that have the names of colors. Which color has the most places associated with it?

4. Use magazines or catalogs to find as many different shades of one season's colors as you can. Either paint or paste those shades to make a color wheel for that season.

5. Make a color wheel of the primary and secondary colors. Choose one of the primary colors and make a list of things that are only that color. Now look at the opposite color on the color wheel and make a list of things that are only that color. Which color has the longer list?

6. Think of at least five phrases that have colors in them and explain what their literal and figurative meanings are. For example, *the color of money* literally means "green" but figuratively means that something is rich or expensive.

7. Make a list of colors. Beside each one, write two adjectives that describe the word for you. For example: yellow—happy, bright. Have someone else make a list, and then compare that list with yours. How many adjectives did you have in common?

8. Defend your view on whether all the old black-and-white movies should be colorized or not. Ask your parents and grandparents how they feel about this issue.
9. What is your favorite color? Tell why.
10. Each season, the fashion and car industries seem to promote certain colors. Look at several sales flyers or catalogs to determine what the colors for this season are. Cut out several and make a color board to show off the colors of this season's fashions or new cars.
11. If you were looking for a certain outfit in a certain color and could not find it, what are some things you could do about your problem?
12. Make a list of industries that have to be very color-conscious.
13. Research colorblindness and give at least five facts about this disability.
14. What things would colorblind people have to compensate for in everyday living? How do you think they handle the problems you have addressed?
15. Do you think the popularity of jeans has anything to do with the fact that they are blue? Explain your answer.
16. Make a list of professions that wear only certain colors. Do you think this list has gotten larger or smaller over the past 25 years? Why?
17. Pretend you are working for a hair product company and they have just put you in charge of coming up with new names for either blondes, brunettes, or redheads. Choose one of these three and come up with at least three names for shades of hair dye that would make people want to have that hair color.
18. Do you think it is wise for crayons to have a scent? Explain your answer.
19. If you could have any job that dealt with colors, what would it be and why?
20. OOPS! A doll made by the company you work for just came off the assembly line with blue hair. You find out there are 10,000 of them. Think of a sales campaign that will sell these dolls.
21. How would you describe the primary colors to a blind person?
22. Is black and white ever better than color? Explain your answer.
23. If you were opening a shop by the name of Colors, what would you be selling? Make a sign that would advertise what you are selling and would attract people to your shop.
24. Do you think it is the color or the shape of flowers that makes people have favorites? Explain your answer.
25. Make a list of things in nature that show all the colors of the rainbow.
26. Some colors will be popular forever, and other colors seem to be very trendy. Make a chart showing some of each.

27. Which car colors are the best? Explain your answers.

28. A salesperson told a homeowner who wanted to sell his house that "vanilla houses sell the fastest!" What do you think the salesperson meant by this statement?

29. What color do you think represents rock'n'roll? What color best represents country music? How about classical music? How about jazz?

30. Should schools be painted bright primary colors or soft pastels? Explain your answer.

31. Explain the difference between *tint* and *shade.*

32. Do you consider black and white to be colors? Explain your answer.

33. An insurance agent told one of her clients that more red cars are involved in accidents than any other color car. Why do you think this is?

34. Can you ever tell the color of something without seeing it? How is this possible?

35. Is autumn prettier than spring in terms of colors? Why or why not?

36. Find out how prisms give off colors. Write or tell someone how it works.

37. Find out what causes a rainbow. Write or tell someone about the information you discovered.

38. Brainstorm a list of books that have the names of colors in the titles. Do you think the colors make the titles better, or do you think it puts off prospective readers? Explain your answer.

39. Draw pictures of the literal meaning of color phrases such as *green with envy.*

40. If you had to give each day of the week a color, which color would you assign each day? Explain your answer.

41. Why do you think phone companies choose yellow pages as opposed to another color? Do they ever use colors other than white or yellow? If so, what for?

42. Choose four holidays and get an index card for each one. For each holiday, draw two or three large squares on the index card. Fill in the squares with colors connnected to that holiday. Show a friend, a classmate, and a family member each index card and ask each person what he or she thinks of when seeing those color combinations. How many people identified the holidays right away? How many answered with something associated with the particular holiday, such as the flag for the 4th of July?

43. Before there were synthetic dyes, nature provided dyes. Give the names of two natural dyes.

44. There are certain symbols that make us think of certain colors. Without giving them any color, draw at least two of these symbols. Ask someone if he or she can tell you what color is associated with each symbol. Color the symbols to see if people get the message quicker. What can you conclude from this?

45. Survey and graph the results of a poll based on this question: "Do you dream in color?"

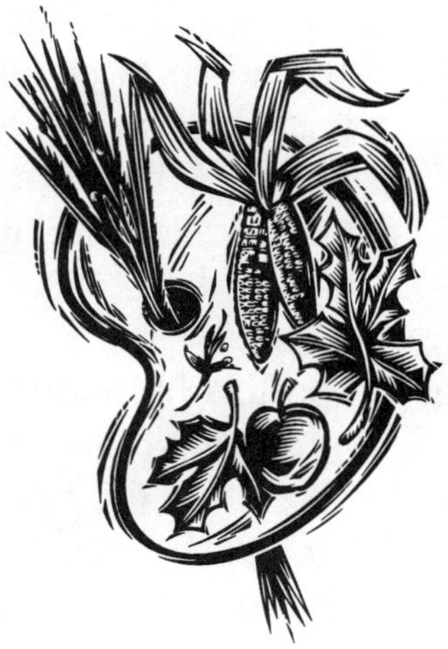

What-Ifs for Fall

Are you looking for a way to get to know your new students better? Would you like to make your students' thinking and writing experiences of the year different, special, and exhilarating? Why not try some "what-ifs"?

All you have to do is present these pages of imagination-provoking ideas and students will do the rest—with enthusiasm! Use the "what-ifs" to start discussions and idea sharing, and then let students' writing flow.

"What-ifs" can also be used to create class newspapers, posters, games, debates, and anything else YOUR imagination allows. Why not ask students . . .

What if . . .

- your school switched its rules—you had vacation in September and October and had to attend school the rest of the year? What would you do with your free time in September and October? What could you do in September and October that you couldn't do before? Would you like this new arrangement? Why or why not?

- you were helping to rake the lawn and for every leaf you raked up, 1,000 more fell in its place? What solutions could you come up with for this problem?

- the governor of your state made a new law stating there would be no more Halloween? Make a list of pros and cons to this situation. What new holiday could you invent to take its place? Think of a new name for your holiday and write a clear description of its customs, decorations, dates to be celebrated, and so on.

- during this hurricane season one particular hurricane named ______ didn't blow trees and houses down but instead blew them up into the sky to fly around indefinitely? What would the sky look like with things floating through it? Draw a picture and write a poem or story to go with it.

- a famous chef asked you to create a fall recipe that no one had ever thought of before? The recipe had to include apples, pumpkins, and potato chips! Write your recipe and the steps necessary to make your concoction, and then describe how and to whom you would serve it. (You may add other strange ingredients, too.)

- you won a contest and on Veterans Day were asked to make a speech in honor of a famous sailor, soldier, or marine from the past or present? For whom would you write the speech? What would you say about him or her? Write your speech.

- you, like Christopher Columbus, became a discoverer? What would you like to discover? Describe the thrill you felt and what you did after making your discovery. Would you want to become famous for your discovery? Why or why not?

- you found yourself sailing on the *Santa Maria* with Christopher Columbus himself? Write some diary entries to describe your daily adventures with this brave explorer. Don't forget to describe how he treated you and how you felt toward him on your voyage together. Who was your best friend on the ship? What were your biggest problems?

- on Labor Day, a holiday to honor all workers and give them a day of rest, virtually EVERY worker in the country stayed home and did absolutely no work? How would your Labor Day celebration be different?

- the pumpkin was on the brink of extinction and there were only 10 left in the country? You are scheduled to go to the only pumpkin farm left to get a pumpkin to carve for Halloween. Would you want to go? Write a letter stating how you feel about getting a pumpkin this year.

- everyone in your class wants to be something scary for Halloween, but you want to be something funny? Describe how you would feel and how you would come to a final decision on what type of costume you would wear.

- it was the fifth day of school for you in a new town and another person who looks just like you and has your name is also new to the school? The teachers keep getting you mixed up and giving you the other person's papers and vice versa. The real mix-up is that the other person's papers are A's and yours are C's. Would you let your teachers know about the confusion or would you keep the A's? How could such a problem be solved?

- at your school's first football game of the season, the star player kicks the first field goal and breaks his foot? You are asked to replace him on the team. Write a diary entry about such a day in your life and how you would feel.

- at your school's first basketball game of the season, the star cheerleader falls from the top of a pyramid formation and is injured for the season? Write a letter to her to cheer her up. What other things would you do to become a good friend to her?

- you are asked by the school's cheerleading coach to write a spirited new school cheer? Write a rhyming cheer and, if you can, sing it to a tune of your choice.

- instead of changing red, yellow, orange, and brown, the autumn leaves began changing pink, blue, lilac, and silver?

- the pumpkin you planted last summer grew taller than your house overnight?

- on the first day of school, you walked into your new classroom and found out that your teacher was your father? your mother? your older sister or brother?

- as you were raking leaves, you found an old key that spoke to you? What would it tell you?

- every day, after school, you walked past a pumpkin patch and noticed one particular pumpkin that already had a face, smiled and winked at you, and called your name?

- every leaf on every oak and maple tree in your neighborhood refused to fall down? The leaves stayed on the trees right through Christmas!

- a squirrel you had been feeding all fall one day walked up to you and said, "Hey, do you have any potato chips instead of nuts?"

- at the school Halloween party, you found every student in your class was wearing the same exact costume as you? What would you say to them? What would you do?

- at your school's open-house meeting, you were asked to make a speech? What would you say?

- on Election Day, in November, a woman was elected President of the United States? How would you feel?

- a witch flew over your school on a broomstick and wrote in smoke, "Hello, _____?" (Put your own name in the blank.) How would you feel? What would you do?

- at the annual Thanksgiving Day parade, you found yourself on the lead float marching

down the avenue? What would your float look like? What would you be wearing or doing?

- as you sat down to Thanksgiving dinner, you found yourself seated next to Pocahontas? What would you say to her?

- on your way to school, a fallen leaf that sparkled like diamonds kept blowing in front of your footsteps? You felt you had to follow wherever it was leading you. Where would it lead you? What would you find?

- a scarecrow you made to scare crows away from your garden ended up making faces at you and was scaring you from going into your own backyard?

- in your trick-or-treat bag, you found a magic gum ball? Every time you chewed it, you were able to finish your homework in three minutes and you knew all answers to all tests. Would you keep chewing it? What if your teacher said there was no gum-chewing in school?

- one bright, crisp fall day, you were picking apples in the orchard? You decided to eat one out of your basket, but as you did, you noticed three more replaced it. Every time you ate an apple, three more appeared in your basket. What would you do? Who would you tell?

What-Ifs for WINTER

Here it is. Winter. What better way to keep warm and keep your students' brain cells cooking than with a sampling of "what-ifs"? Let your students' imaginations flow, their verbal skills stay finely tuned, and their creativity flourish on a cold winter's day with these activities.

There are so many things you can do with "what-ifs": write stories, conduct discussions in the form of news broadcasts or debates and plays, compose songs, and write and illustrate poems.

The possibilities are endless, and it all starts with a little "what-if."

What if . . .

- at midnight on New Year's Eve, you found yourself back in the year 1920 or 1950? What things would you see? What things would you hear and do? (You might wish to consult parents, grandparents, and history books to find out a little more about the particular time period you have chosen.)

- at midnight on New Year's Eve, the clock struck the year 2099? What new sights might you see? What new activities might you take part in?

- at your own New Year's Eve party, you chose to wear a shiny, very special sparkling hat? When you placed it on your head, you turned into Father Time and found yourself in charge of controlling time all over the world. What kinds of things would you do with your power?

- for the new year you were ordered by law to make one and only one New Year's resolution? If you did not fulfill the resolution, you would have to pay harsh penalties. What resolution would you choose? How would you go about making sure you stuck to it?

- on New Year's Day you discovered you had the power to read people's minds? Whose mind would you most want to read? Why? Whose mind would you least want to read? Why?

- for your January ski trip, you invented special skis that would enable you to reach the bottom of a ski slope faster than anyone else around? Draw your special invention. Would you keep your skis a secret or would you share your invention with others?

- on February 1 the principal of your school announced at an assembly that school was over for the year? What would you do with your time from February until next September?

- on February 14, Valentine's Day, a six-foot-high valentine card was delivered to your door, bearing only the message, "Let's be best friends"? Who do you wish had sent you such a card?

- for Valentine's Day, everyone in your school was told to wear red? What color would you wear? Why?

- you received a box of 12 chocolates, but inside each was not a sweet filling but a note about an event that would come true in your lifetime? What would you want the 12 messages to be?

- you could win a four-year college scholarship by creating a recipe for a unique winter soup? What ingredients would you put in your soup? Write your unique recipe and illustrate it if possible.

- you were drinking a steamy mug of hot chocolate, and your little sister or brother dropped a marshmallow into your drink, but instead of melting, the marshmallow began to puff up? Before you knew it, it filled up your whole bedroom. What will happen next?

- it had been a bad winter, with 12 blizzards, and you couldn't stand to see another flake of snow? You wanted it to melt. Invent and illustrate a contraption that will melt all snow. Describe your invention in detail.

- it was Super Bowl Sunday and you were chosen from everyone in the country to write a cheer for your favorite team? How would your cheer sound?

- halfway through the ice-hockey season, the major teams in your area decided to use something else instead of the traditional puck to finish out the season? What else could your favorite team use instead of a puck to play hockey with? Draw a cartoon of a team using the new equipment.

- at your holiday dinner, instead of having turkey with traditional stuffing, you found turkey with a 100-foot-long noodle on your plate?

- instead of snowing snowflakes in December, it began to snow oatmeal, lemon drops, or bubblegum?
- as you were curled up in front of the fireplace, gazing into a brightly glowing fire, you began to see a dancing nutcracker, just like in the famous ballet?
- you found only one gift for Hanukkah, but it was in a huge 100" x 100" box? What might it be?
- you found only one gift under the Christmas tree and it was no bigger than your little toe? What might it be?
- Mrs. Claus was declaring her equal rights and demanded to accompany Santa on his magical flight?
- Mrs. Claus demanded not only to ride in the sleigh but also to drive the sleigh?
- someone played a practical joke on Santa and stole his special fur-trimmed red suit? What else might he wear?
- you were walking in the mall on a busy shopping Saturday and a little boy in front of you dropped a $50 billl? What would you do?
- Santa was tired of saying, "Ho, Ho, Ho"? What might he say instead?
- every store in your state was out of all types of bags, boxes, and wrapping paper? What would you use to wrap your gifts?
- it was 40° below zero and it was too cold for Frosty the Snowman to stand outside? What if he marched through the front door of your house in order to warm up? What would you say to him? What would you do with him?
- you received magic mittens as a gift? When you put them on your hands, you could touch anyone and make him or her your best friend. Who would you touch?
- at a holiday party, a huge piñata was broken by screaming children and out popped a ___________?
- Santa's four-foot-tall elves drank a magic potion and began to grow? First they grew to 5 feet, then 6 feet, then on and on until they were 10 feet tall! What would Santa do?
- you were on a ski trip and you discovered that you had the only pair of skis on Earth that skied UP mountains instead of down mountains?
- while baking holiday cookies, you sprinkled them with shiny little candies? When they came out of the oven, you found out the candies had turned to real jewels. What would you do with the cookies?

What-Ifs

for

SPRING

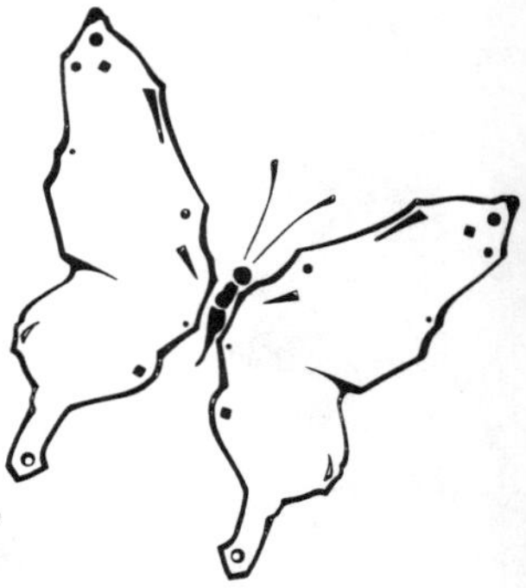

After you get to know "what-ifs," I'm sure you too will be able to think of many exciting uses for them.

What if . . .

- a newly hatched hummingbird weighed 10 pounds?
- a brilliant scarlet tulip popped out of the ground and grew three feet per day for seven days? What would you do with a 21-foot tulip?
- the newborn birds were so happy it was spring that they sang 24 hours a day under your bedroom window and wouldn't stop?
- spring just wouldn't come to your town and it kept snowing right through August?
- as you were on an egg hunt, you found a 300-pound milk chocolate egg?
- a baby bunny hopped onto your head and wouldn't leave?

- a mother robin found out she had just hatched chickens?
- a bright orange-and-black butterfly followed you everywhere, including to school?
- a new pair of spring shoes made you walk backward whenever you wore them?
- a new spring hat you bought made you smarter than your mom or dad every time you put it on?
- the circus came to town and the ringmaster asked YOU to be the star of it? What would your act be?
- on a visit to the beach, you built a sandcastle with magic sand that allowed you to enter the castle and become a king, queen, or princess for a day?
- one night you were able to catch all of the bats in your neighborhood? What would you do with them?
- you were chosen to be the leader of an Easter parade and you had the power to lead the whole parade anywhere at all? Where would you take it?
- the water in a nearby lake or river turned to ice? to maple syrup? to fruit juice?
- you discovered a waterfall in a secret place in your own backyard?
- you won a trip to a wonderful island but you found out you could only take one other person with you? Who would it be?
- you and your family went on a wonderful trip together and when you got to your destination and unpacked your bags, you found everything you packed shrunk to baby sizes?
- one warm spring night as you gazed up at the stars, you saw your teacher float by on the back of a flying horse?

Now that you know the powers of "what-ifs," you can make up your own and do whatever you want with them. Don't forget, wherever you go and whatever you do, there's always a what-if waiting for you!

What-ifs for SUMMER

Summer is a perfect time for kicking back, relaxing, and letting the imagination run wild. While children are gazing up at stars and fireflies on hot summer nights or sitting by a cool pool on sizzling summer days, a what-if can make the difference between ordinary hot weather fun and extraordinary summer delight!

Have children think about what-ifs carefully, then talk about them freely. Then watch the creative fireworks really begin. Stories and poems can be written, dialogues for mini plays can be created, pictures can be drawn, and even inventions can be made from one simple what-if. Just think of all the creativity that will take place with more than one!

What if . . .

- you're perched at the highest point of a Ferris wheel gently swinging back and forth? As you look down, you see not one single other person below in the entire amusement park. Where could everyone be? What might have happened?

- you jump into your pool and it's too, too cold? That's because you haven't jumped into water! Your pool is filled with millions of tiny ice cubes. How did they get there? What will you do next?

- at a carnival you win an adorable, lime-green stuffed frog? You bring it home and put it beside your bed, when suddenly it begins to talk to you! What does it say? What do you say? Write a dialogue between the two of you.

- at an amusement park your friend plays a trick on you? He or she buys you cotton candy, but when you bite into it, you realize it's real cotton! Now what (harmless) trick could you play on this friend?

- on a camping trip you are the only one who can't make the tent stay up? Invent and draw something you could sleep in instead of a tent.

- you're at the beach gathering shells? You look down and find a topaz ring that fits you perfectly. Write an adventure story about what you go through with this find. Will you keep it? Will you go on an extensive search to find its owner?

- you're at the beach building an elaborate sandcastle? When you've finally put on the finishing touch, a miniature animated king and queen appear! Make up an exciting adventure about your magical kingdom and its rulers. Are they a good or bad king and queen? What will you do with them?

- from the beach you're looking out at the sea and suddenly a huge sailing vessel appears? On it, you see Babe the pig and Porky the pig. Write a conversation you overhear between the two of them.

- at a Fourth of July picnic, the mayor of your town asks you to make a speech about what freedom means to you? Write your speech.

- a major toy company has hired you to design a new kind of yo-yo, a new way of playing jacks, a one-of-a-kind jump rope, or a unique pool toy? Design and describe your new toys. Name them, too!

- your school principal asks you to write a letter to the President of the United States, asking him to be a guest speaker for the first day of school in September? Write your letter. How would you persuade the President that he *must* come for the visit?

- you have a pool party on the Fourth of July and are allowed to invite any two famous people in the world? Who would you invite? Create special invitations you would send to these two people. When they got to your party, what would you say to them? Make up a diary entry describing how your party went.

- you are asked by a well-known ice-cream company to create a new holder for ice cream? It cannot be a cone, cup, or bowl of any kind. What would you invent? Draw it and name it. Design a magazine ad that will help sell your new creation.

- you stayed in the sun too long, but instead of getting a sunburn or tan, you look down at your arms and legs and find out you're striped? How would you feel? What would you do about it?

- while camping out one starry summer night, you see a rather large firefly? It can talk and has asked you to follow it to a secret, magical place. Would you go? If you went, what would you see and do? (Don't forget, this is only pretend.)

- you were asked by major sports stars to make up a totally new kind of game? It must be a combination of basketball, baseball, and tennis! Describe your game, including the rules, in detail. Now try playing your unique game.

- for one day this summer, you are allowed to work at any job you want, and you will get paid for it? What would you want to do? Write a poem or song about your day on this job.

- there is no more electrical power left in the world? You are asked to invent a new way to keep cool in the summer. Design and illustrate your invention.

- there is a contest in your town for which you could win a trip to Europe? You must pack a picnic basket full of never-before-heard-of summer foods. List five or more unique summer foods that could win the contest. Try writing recipes for some of them.

- your dad or mom has opened a new restaurant in your town? You are in charge of making up the menu. Design a menu, complete with prices. Make it different from any other menu you have ever seen.

- at an outdoor concert, you are asked to go up on stage to sing? You are thrilled to do it. What would you sing? Why that song? Now sing it!

- you received a magical camera as a gift? Every time you take a picture with it, everything or everyone in the photo multiplies by 10! What would you want to take photos of all summer? What would you definitely *not* take photos of?

By now you've seen that a "what-if" is a short little phrase with some pretty big power. "What-ifs" are always with you. Just look around this summer at people and things in a little different manner and you will have a "what-if" brewing! Stay cool and have fun!

What Would You Do If . . . ?

Use your imagination! Brainstorm at least three solutions for each of the problems below. You might want to create unusual responses, or you may use very sensible and logical answers. What would you do if . . .

1. you woke up and found your head was invisible? The doorbell rings and you see through the window that it is your best friend.

2. you find yourself locked in an ice-cream shop in the mall and all the electricity went out?

3. you were chosen to be the first person to travel back in time?

4. you had the ability to communicate with cats and dogs?

5. you were asked to interview your favorite sports star?

What-Ifs?

Think about some of the "what-ifs" listed below. Do you get a picture in your brain of what each scenario might be? This is called creative visualizing! Read each "what-if" and decide what you are thinking. Draw a picture with each description.

What if . . .

you could stretch your body any way you wanted?

you had a computerized pencil that would know how to do all your homework?

you had a secret pet that was an elephant?

your shoes had special laser attachments?

you won two million dollars?

your bed had a jet engine hooked up to it?

you looked in the bathtub and found it filled with gelatin?

you could travel to another planet for vacation?

your dentist used invisible tools?

Can you write some "what-ifs" of your own? Give them to classmates and start a scrapbook of "what-if" ideas!

What Would You Do If . . .?

Select one of the scenarios below. Use your imagination and think about what you would do if this really happened! Write a story, prepare a speech, or create a comic strip showing your solution.

What if . . .

- 300 mice had just gotten out of their cages in a pet shop where you worked?
- you were locked into your favorite department store overnight?
- you woke up one morning to find yourself turned into an adult?
- you were able to communicate with animals?
- you could travel into the future? into the past?
- you worked in a chocolate factory and the air conditioning just broke down?
- someone just gave you one million dollars?
- your pet frog just won a national hopping contest?
- a character in your favorite book just came alive?
- you just won a hippopotamus in a contest you entered?
- all the electricity in the world just stopped?
- you could travel any place in the world for free?
- the dinner served to you in a fancy restaurant came with a fly in the mashed potatoes?
- you met a robot at the grocery store?
- you could buy a homework machine?

Alien Edition

New Planet Discovered and Presented to ____________________

A new planet, rather like planet Earth, has been discovered and presented to a fine local student. This planet will be in excellent hands with the knowledge and expertise of the new owner. The new owner will help plan the government, rules, regulations, life forms, continents, and other components of life on the new planet. We congratulate the new owner and offer full assistance in helping start a perfect new planet!

____________________ became the new owner when ____

____. The new owner was selected due to such wonderful background in the areas of: ____________________

____

________________, and ____________________.

As head of the new government, ____________ has suggested the following: ____________________

____

My Planet Looks Like This

____

____

____

____

____

____

____

____

____

Inside This Issue

1 New Life Forms
2 New Government
3 New Planet Map
4 Patriotic Symbols
5 Rules and Regulations
6 Geographical Characteristics

Life forms that reside on the new planet are called ____________

Our Fearless New Leader and President of the Planet

An Average Citizen of Planet Perfect

A ____________ for Planet Perfect

A ____________ for Planet Perfect

Map of Planet Perfect

Information about climate and weather on this planet:

Patriotic Symbols for Planet Perfect

Flag

Anthem

Planet Flower

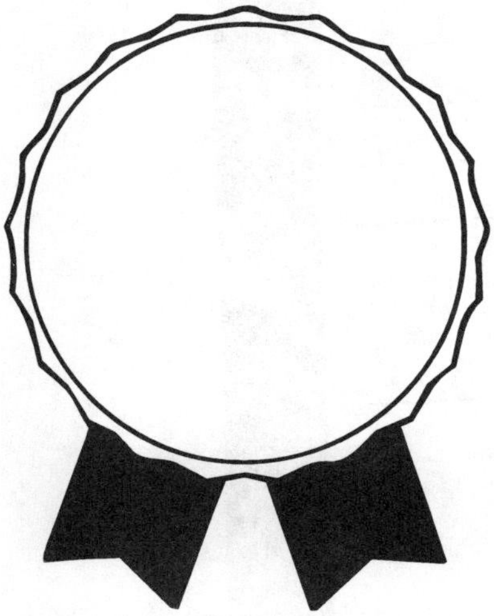

Planet Bird

Planet Tree

Information about the patriotic symbols of Planet Perfect:

Rules and Regulations for Planet Perfect

Think, Write, and Draw

You Are an Explorer!

Name(s) of your crew: ____________________

Name of your vessel: ____________________

Where are you going? ____________________

Why are you going there?

____

List the supplies you need to take on your expedition.

____

____

____

____

____

____

____

____

____

____

What are the dates of your expedition? __________

When do you hope to return? __________

Draw a map of where you are going.
Include all the landforms that you know exist.

1. You have arrived! How long did it take to get here? ______________________

____

2. What are some problems you encountered on your trip and how did you solve them?

____

____

____

____

____

____

____

____

____

____

____

3. What did you find? Describe the people, vegetation, animals, climate, and so on.

____

____

____

____

____

____

4. What did you bring as gifts?

____

____

____

5. Are the natives friendly? What do they offer you?

____

____

____

Draw a picture of you with the natives. Make sure to include housing, flora, and fauna.

Draw a map of your new discovery. Name the landforms and water systems your expedition has revealed.

Prepare your initial report about what you experienced on your journey. Be sure to include facts about your travels—what you saw, how you felt, and what you discovered.

Future Reflections of Me

It's the year 2025 and this is your life . . .

Think ahead to the year 2025. What will your life be like in the future? What type of job will you have? What will your family be like? What type of house will you be living in and where will you be living? What kind of vehicle will you be driving? What type of things do you see yourself doing during your free time in the future? How do you see yourself in the year 2025? Play a game of time travel forward into the future. Make a few predictions based on what you think the future will be like and what it holds for you in particular. Do the following activities based on how you see yourself when you become your parents' age.

Professional Advertisement

Design an advertisement for the job you will hold in the future. Make a logo integrating the name of your company and add a catchy slogan. Use colors that make a statement about the type of company you work for.

My name is ____,

and in the year 2025 I will be __________ years old.

The headline news for this date in 2025 will look like this:

The World Tribune

And tonight we honor . . .

You have just received information that you are to be given an award. Think about why you will be receiving that award based on how you see yourself in the future. You could receive the award for something you have done in your profession or for something you have done in your community. You can receive the award for something you have created or for something you have done that is heroic, or even for something you found you are good at as a hobby. You decide.

I am receiving the award for

Explain what the requirements are for receiving this award.

Explain why you are the perfect candidate for this award.

Design the award you will be receiving.

(It can be a medal, trophy, certificate, plaque, and so on.)

Who will be presenting the award? ____________________

Where will the award be presented? ____________________

Whom will you be taking to see you receive this award? ____________________

Does anything special accompany this award (such as money, title, vacation, and so on)? If so, tell what and be specific.

____

____

____

____

____

Awards Committee

You have been asked to fax the following information. Please fill in the blanks and return to the Awards Committee as soon as possible. Please feel free to add any additional information you would like.

____________________ lives with ____________________
full name — can be general or specific

____________________ in ____________________.
continue with people you live with — place

____________________ completed the ________ grade in school.
first name

____________________ received a ____________________
He or *She* — *diploma* or *degree*

from ____________________ in ____________ .
educational institution — year

____________________ has worked as a ____________________
He or *She* — list types of jobs you have held

for ____________. ____________________ is now working as a
number of years — name

____________________ for ____________________.
position title — company name

____________________ job requires ____________________ to
His or *Her* — name

____________________. In ____________________ spare time,
do what types of work — *his* or *her*

____________________ likes to ____________________.
name — do what types of pastimes

Provide the following information for a picture board to be displayed the night of the awards.

Family Photo: Include names and ages of everyone in the picture. List them from left to right.

Photo of Home: Give location.

Provide the following information for a picture board to be displayed the night of the awards.

Photo of Vehicle or Favorite Mode of Transportation: Give vanity plate.

Photo of Candidate During Leisure Time Doing Hobby or Favorite Pastime.

January

Monday	Tuesday	Wednesday	Thursday	Friday
Think about what, how, where, and when you study best. Are there any patterns?	Combine a paper clip and a ribbon. 	Are we becoming more of a listening society than a reading society? Ask some adults.	After reading a section, relax and form vivid mind pictures of what you have read. Exaggerate!	Make connections between your spelling words and your home life.
How many ways can you think of to study for your next test?	What are prompts? How can they be useful?	List types of tests and reasons why tests are taken.	List reasons why you want to make good grades. 	How can you predict what a teacher expects you to learn?
	How is memorizing like dancing?	Think up some "What if" questions that relate to events from your current social studies topic.	Create a personally productive study motto.	Which is more important, listening or speaking?
Think up many ways to study a spelling list.	How could you make a school desk more comfortable?	Create a test-study game of answers. A partner must present appropriate questions.	Invent a new memorizing device.	Combine a funnel and an umbrella. 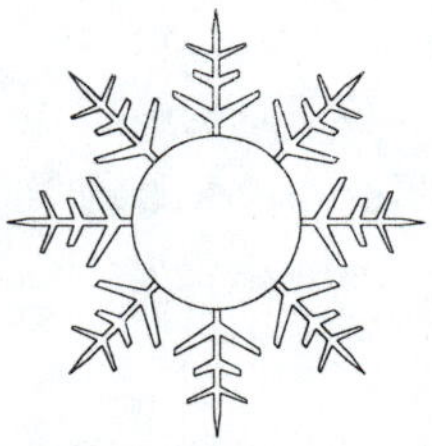
List things adults must memorize.	Combine a snowflake and a raindrop.	How does an item in today's news relate to your current science topic?	How does this week's spelling list relate to your current social studies topic?	What would happen if all the tests in the world were abandoned?

Just Think . . .

February

Monday	Tuesday	Wednesday	Thursday	Friday
List 10 people to whom you have recently listened. Evaluate your ability to listen to each one of them.	Think of ways to relax before taking a test. 	Create a set of typical test question words such as *compare* and *explain*.	Invent a personal acronym to use for a studying slogan. Design a banner.	What effect would color highlighting have on your note-taking? Try it.
How can studying be creative?	How does this week's math relate to your current science topic?	Change the color of roads.	Invent a game to play with a partner to remember information for a test.	Invent a new note-taking system. 
Survey several adults about the most recent test they have taken.	Set up some criteria to judge radio commercials. Listen to a few and rate their effectiveness.	Visualize each of your spelling words in a very elaborate scene.	Can you connect something from this week's reading to your current social studies topic?	Predict new ways students will study 200 years from now.
How is studying like a tomato? Relate the phrase *Divide and conquer* to studying.	With your class, create a test-taker's guide.	List reasons why people fail tests. 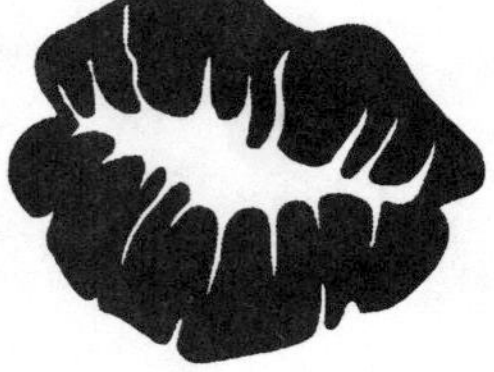	What can tests prove? How has studying changed throughout history?	Make a list of all the things about which you would like to learn.
How is school like a balancing act?	Categorize in four different ways a list of words you must study.	Invent ways you can make listening to boring lectures more interesting.	Survey 20 people to get immediate reactions to the word test. Interpret results.	Imagine a world with only circular things. Write, draw, or tell about it.

March

Monday	Tuesday	Wednesday	Thursday	Friday
Create a new motto for your country.	How is an ocean like a rock concert? 	How is a person like a bridge?	What makes a good vacation spot?	*Twelve* is the answer. What was the question?
Combine two things to make a better automobile.	How can you tell when conflict is happening?	Invent a first toy for a baby.	Create a code that uses colors. 	Design a better clock.
List ways to wake up a sleepyhead.	Categorize roads in at least six different ways.	In how many ways can you use a skateboard?	Compare pillows and puddles.	List the biggest things in the world.
Invent a new style of suitcase. 	Be a flower bulb. Visualize your life.	Which day of the week is most valuable?	Combine a brush and a hook.	Think up a new way to classify the books in the library.
Which people are most important?	Invent a new day of the week.	Which is easier, a push or a pull? 	List things that are better as they get older.	Picture a noisy yet wonderful scene. What do you see?

April

Monday	Tuesday	Wednesday	Thursday	Friday
Compare a balloon and marshmallow.	Invent a new kind of candy bar.	Be a professional photographer. Tell about five things you'll be sure to shoot.	How's a house like a costume? 	Combine a boot and a shovel.
What makes a poem good? What is a poem?	Compare a desk and a car.	Classify all the green things you see today.	What makes a good friend?	List your favorite things to think about.
Classify man-made things. 	Compare seeing and hearing.	What if everyone had a twin?	Your town needs a new library. Design it.	Be a kite. Take a wild and windy trip. 
Invent a better mailbox.	Tell about your life as a penny.	Combine a submarine and an airplane.	How can you tell when it's been a good day?	List things that go bump in the night.
Classify the people at your school.	In what ways could you get to the top of a flagpole?	What color is success? Why? 	Create a new ice-cream flavor.	Who would you trade places with? Why?

Just Think . . .

May

Monday	Tuesday	Wednesday	Thursday	Friday
List reasons for cloud watching. 	What's good about night?	Compare a ridge to something alive.	Classify people's names in several ways.	In what ways can you protect yourself while staying home alone?
List ways to keep cool.	Compare a test and a roller coaster ride.	Combine two wooden things to make something new.	Visualize a crowded scene. Make it change. Make it non-human.	What makes people happy? 
Which is heavier, an A or an F? 	Tell about two of the happiest people you know.	Invent new uses for carpeting. 	Combine TV with something else to create a great new product.	Where do you find stripes?
Classify athletes other than by their sports.	Compare something old to something soft. How are your two chosen items alike?	What makes a good book title? Think up five winners for new book titles.	How is a test like a table? 	Visualize some popping scenes. Can you hear them as well as see them?
Invent some new spy devices. 	Change notebooks to make them better.	What is conflict? Is it ever good?	List 20 words that begin with K. Now classify them.	What would a notebook say to a student?

Just Think . . .

June

Monday	Tuesday	Wednesday	Thursday	Friday
Connection is the answer. What is the question?	Which is calmer, lettuce or broccoli? 	What vegetable does your teacher remind you of?	What things might a shoe say?	Compare *left and right.*
How would you choose the winner of the Best Joker Award?	In what ways can students show patriotism?	Picture a celebration in your mind.	Invent a boredom preventer. 	Classify a day's time in several different ways.
Combine two or more ingredients to make a better breakfast cereal.	Compare a picture and a thousand words.	*Soup* is the answer. What was the question?	How is a student like a blender?	Picture in your mind a deserted town. Tell about it.
Compare *in and out.*	When is remembering easy?	List things a farmer might say.	Use your mental camera to snap pictures of water scenes.	Can you discover many famous people whose last names are colors?
Picture a muddy situation. Put yourself into it.	List reasons for a hole. 	When is forgetting hard?	Invent a crying-baby husher.	How does a person achieve greatness?

July

Monday	Tuesday	Wednesday	Thursday	Friday
What are some new ways to catch fish?	Tell things a dinosaur might say. 	List things a mother might say.	Change a cereal box to make it better.	Draw a picture of your mom's favorite shoes.
Why do we have holidays?	What categories can you think of for boxes?	What makes a good movie?	Think of things to do with ice. 	Invent a self-watering system for plants.
Change stamps to make them better.	Be a spoon. Tell about it. 	What is the hardest thing you must do?	Which is smarter, up or down?	Think of categories for cards.
In the eyes of a parent, what are six dangerous things a child might do?	List things to do with an egg.	Invent a better bag for potato chips.	Combine something slimy and something dry.	Picture a package. What's inside?
What things might a dog say?	In the eyes of a child, what are six dangerous things to do?	What if Abraham Lincoln lived today? 	What if Hansel and Gretel didn't like candy?	How might things be different if the U.S. were half its size?

Just Think . . .

August

Monday	Tuesday	Wednesday	Thursday	Friday
Which is slower, a twist or a twirl?	Draw a picture of Mr. Grump. 	Combine a packet of seeds and a clown.	Find a picture showing balance.	Take a mind trip to your closet. What's there?
Who is most important in your life?	Classify the contents of your desk.	What is expensive?	List crooked things. 	Invent a new kind of umbrella.
Combine weeds and cages.	Get inside an ice cube in your mind. Tell about your cold trip.	How can people learn to spell more easily?	Classify things in your refrigerator.	Rank 10 foods from sweet to sour.
How is a sweater like your favorite relative?	List things to do with a newspaper. 	Create a new container for toothpaste.	Combine a boat and a gorilla.	See the moving things in your house. List them.
When should people apologize?	Invent something to scratch with.	List absorbent things.	The money is gone. Where did it go?	

Just Think . . .

September

Monday	Tuesday	Wednesday	Thursday	Friday
What is the difference between a goal and a wish?	Would you rather be a tooth or a nail?	List things or rewards that make people work. 	What roles do you play in your life? Rank them in some way.	List some of the goals your parents have for you.
Create a wish list for an ant. 	How does fear relate to goal setting?	List three special goals for yourself.	Create a poster for your personal goals.	How is a goal like a piece of glass? 
Find a picture of harmony. 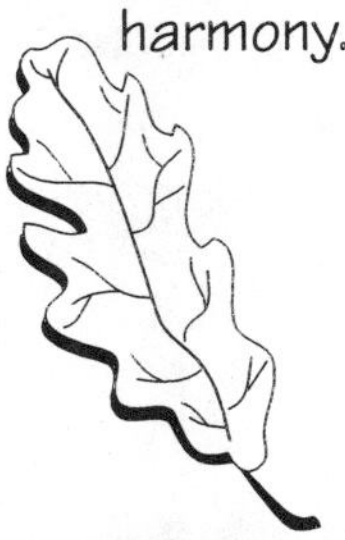	Visualize your "route" to goal #1. What will be the first step? Next? Record the pictures.	Habits are hard to break. Create 10 ways to break a very stubborn habit.	List some bad habits a fish might have.	List 10 decisions you recently made.
How is a decision like a drawbridge?	Compare typical adult and child goals.	In what ways can you tell if your goals are realistic?	Make up a class goal. Make up a cheer to encourage the group.	Combine a top and a bottom. 
What makes goals most likely to be achieved? 	Think of some unique "reminders" for goal achievement.	List some difficult choices for someone your age.	List ways to catch a falling star.	Draw two pictures. Draw one of activity and one of achievement.

Just Think . . .

October

Monday	Tuesday	Wednesday	Thursday	Friday
What goals do local political candidates have for your city? Categorize and compare.	When is work play? When is play work?	Predict your teacher's goals for your class this month.	Compare gardening to dancing. 	Define *problem*. Define it visually.
Find five problems. Match them up with people who have expertise to assist.	Describe several problems a sidewalk might have. 	Show how a sentence is like a building.	Would you rather be a sponge or a magnet?	How is a goal like an egg?
List goals people may have. Categorize them.	Find some pictures of famous people to match some of yesterday's goals.	Survey 10 adults for their top two goals. Tally and graph results. Predict what others would say.	Make up some goals for an inanimate object of your choice. 	What is a support group? Visualize many different support groups.
Think up needs of people in your school. What goals could come from your needs list?	In what ways do you control your life?	Picture a plan in some way. 	What do questions and cats have in common?	Design a goal-assistance machine.
Why do plans get changed? 	Show in picture form a plan that got changed.	Compare a smorgasbord and a system.	Decide on your #1 goal. What made you choose it?	How is a pencil like a drill?

Just Think . . .

November

Monday	Tuesday	Wednesday	Thursday	Friday
List ways to tell time. 	List and prioritize your current "to do's."	Which is more effective, reward or punishment?	What is the difference between a deadline and a goal?	List ways people procrastinate.
What is over the rainbow?	What do you think is on your teacher's priority list today?	Which things on your parents' "to do" list could you do?	List things you do frequently. Which take the most time? Analyze.	Make a "to do" list for a famous person. Prioritize it. 
Create a new way to remind people of the essential tasks for the day.	Would you rather be a pencil or a paper? 	List possible teacher reactions to a late assignment.	Visualize an organized working place for yourself. What do you see?	List decisions you made last week. Rank them in order of difficulty.
Compare goals and tasks.	List decisions a parent must make.	What is under the bed? 	*Decision making* is the answer. What is the question?	List priorities for a particular animal. Be very creative.
What did the boat say to the water? 	List things that take years to complete.	If you completed all your responsibilities for a month, what would you do with all your time?	What rewards would you give yourself for completing tasks?	Categorize ways people your age spend time.

Just Think . . .

December

Monday	Tuesday	Wednesday	Thursday	Friday
Are there any universal family goals humans maintain?	List 10 things you wish you could do. 	Compare deadlines and pine trees.	Locate information on some "risk takers." Decide when risk taking is good.	Compare excellence and perfection.
Create a better way to organize the school day or school year.	Analyze occupations for the amount of spontaneity required.	Collect data from people about the amount of planning they do in their daily lives.	What did silver say to black? 	Is the art of memorization important?
What are some interruptions you have that get in the way of your work?	List ways to deal with interruptions when you are working.	Which is better, routine or spontaneity?	Locate an appropriate quotation for a procrastinator.	Which month is the heaviest?
Invent a new technique for evaluating student work.	Analyze the mistakes on several papers you have completed. Why did you make them?	Relate the tasks you completed in school to the adult world, to the animal world, and to the world of a baby.	What if our system of measuring time were changed?	Is creativity always desired? 
Discuss "the right answer." 	Categorize ways people deal with failure.	List things that change a great deal over a long period of time.	Invent a new time system for our world.	In what ways could you convince people to adopt your new time system?